GarethGates
Talking Point

Gareth Gates with Gavin Reeve

To all my fans – your continued support is appreciated so much and I love you loads. You are, without doubt, the best fans out there and you are as big a part of what I am today as me!

To my friends and family – thank you for being there for me no matter what and for your guidance and love.

Lots of love **Gareth**

First published in Great Britain in 2003 by **Virgin Books Ltd,** Thames Wharf Studios, Rainville Road, London W6 9HA. Copyright © **19 Merchandising Limited** 2003. The right of GarethGates to be identified as the Author of this Work has been asserted by him in accordance with the Copyright, Designs and Patents Act, 1988.

A catalogue record for this book is available from the British Library. ISBN 1 85227 009 8
Printed and bound in Great Britain by Butler & Tanner.
Photographs by Kate Martin.
Additional photographs: 14-15, 16, 17, 18, 19, 20, 21, 22, 23, 25, 52, 54-55, 56 (top): Jeff Spicer / Alpha; 41 (top L): Ken McKay / Rex Features; 41 (top R): Rex Features; 41 (bottom L): Julian Makey / Rex Features; 41 (bottom R), 44 (R), 53, 56 (bottom): David Fisher / LFI; 43: Marc Larkin / LFI; 44 (L): Richard Crampton / Rex Features; 46: Action Press / Rex Features.

Design by **EgelnickandWebb**.com.

acknowledgements

I'd like to thank Mum, Dad, Nicola, Charlotte and Jessica. Also Simon Fuller, Kelly (and her claw!), Charl, Lucy, Ollie, Maya and everyone at 19. Also thanks to everyone at Virgin Books, Kate Martin and Andy (for putting up with my face all day at the shoot!), also to Gavin (for making me sound intelligent!), Ben Mohapi, Ben Mohapi, Ben Mohapi (coz I know he wants to be famous!), Faye Sawyer and baby girl. Lastly a big thanks to all my adorable fans.

contents

foreword   04

introduction   06

Chapter One   it's good to talk   08

Chapter Two   on the road   14

Chapter Three   family, friends and girlfriends   26

Chapter Four   celebrity   34

Chapter Five   my fans   42

Chapter Six   charity begins at home   50

Chapter Seven   international   58

Chapter Eight   music   66

Chapter Nine   chips and kickboxing

                   – bits of chat with Gareth   74

                   afterword   80

foreword

I dedicate this book to all my fans. Your constant support and love is so much appreciated. I hope you all enjoy it – an update on what life has been like for the past year or so and a bit of an insight into what goes on when you're in the public eye!

Of course I've been doing a bit of posing too – there are loads of new photos of me which I hope you'll like. I'm having the best time and have really settled into the writing, singing and travelling that's involved in the job, so thanks so much for helping me fulfil my dream.

I look forward to seeing you soon. In the meantime, take care and enjoy the book.

With love,

Jareth x

'It's good to be able to talk about everything that's happened, and **where my head is at right now.** *When I look back* **it's incredible to think of everything I've experienced,** *sometimes* **it doesn't seem real'**

GARETH, JUNE 2003

A guy from Bradford came second in a talent contest and captured the nation's hearts with his angelic voice, his classic good looks and his stammer. He sold over 3.2 million singles in the UK alone, over 700,000 copies of his debut album, over 250,000 copies of his first book, has been on two sell-out tours, starred (briefly) in a film, helped raise millions of pounds for charity, been linked with various women in the tabloids and also changed his hairstyle. Is that the end of the story? No way. This is just the beginning...

it's good to talk

When you interview Gareth, he always has a pen and a pad with him. When he gets stuck on a word or phrase, he writes it down, which seems to jog his speech. Subsequently the conversation flows smoothly, and you end up with sheets of paper covered in words like 'raw', 'sexy' and 'relationship'. There are doodles too. Gareth is just as likely to draw something as write it. Whether it's a near-death experience or the comparative sizes of northern and southern scampi, Gareth will sketch it out. Celebrity Pictionary at its finest.

'The stammer is still there, even though in my mind I imagine a time when it will be gone completely'

The stammer is still there, even though in my mind I imagine a time when it will be gone completely. At the moment it goes in waves; I have good days and I have bad days. When I've got time to work on it and do the special exercises that I'm supposed to do, it gets a bit better. It makes a difference if I'm relaxed, then it's better. If I'm talking about certain subjects, or if I'm put on the spot, it gets worse. If I've had a drink, it can go either way. It can make it really amazing, like 'blah-blah-blah-blah-blah-blah', or it can make it ten times worse. It'll be a complete block. Nothing. Which is hard, because if you're out and you're talking to someone, especially a girl, and you stop talking completely…

I suppose I could practise a few chat-up lines, or just be more physical. Be like, 'Hi', then just grab them! No, it's not really me…

To be fair, it used to be really hard, because I had to say my name, and I couldn't say anything, or I started to speak and stammer and they were, like, 'What's going on, what kind of bloke have I pulled?' Now everyone knows I've got a stammer, and everyone knows my name, so it makes it easier. They expect me to stammer.

It does make me listen a lot though, rather than talk about myself. A lot of girls like that. I'm a really good listener. My name, Gareth, is Welsh, and it means 'a good ear to confide in'. I don't know which ear it is though! I'm one of those people that people tell stuff to. I get to hear about everything. It's like, 'Why are you telling me this?'

'Gareth is Welsh: it means "a good ear to confide in"'

Because of the way my speech is at the minute, acting's something I hadn't really thought about, but I was chuffed when S Club asked me to be in their movie, *Seeing Double*. It wasn't really a starring role – in fact I only went to the set twice! Once was to do the end scene on the beach, once to do the earlier bit in the castle. The first time I was there, I just looked around and thought, 'What am I doing here?' S Club had all acted before, what with their TV show, but that was my first ever taste of acting. Saying that, it was hardly acting. I didn't say much, just walked on, did it and walked off.

I was absolutely gutted when I saw the finished film though. Not because it's rubbish or anything, but because of my hair! When we filmed the end shot, I'd finally managed to persuade Ben, my hairdresser, to get rid of the spikes and change it to the way it is now. But in the film they airbrushed my hair to make it look like I had spikes again, and it looks absolutely pathetic. When it comes out on video, look at the end of it and you'll see. They made it really zig-zaggy! When I saw it I was like, 'What is that?' I went to see it at the pictures with a load of people. I was nearly shouting, 'Look at my hair! Look what they've done!' Some poor bloke or woman must have spent hours retouching my hair. I reckon my hair must have come under the special effects budget!

Doing the film was a nice distraction, because the rest of the time has been taken up with touring, promotion, Comic Relief and recording the new album. It's been non-stop, but I don't mind a bit; this is what I've always wanted to do, and now I'm doing it. It's good to be able to talk about everything that's happened and where my head is at right now. When I look back, it's incredible to think of everything that's happened to me. Sometimes it doesn't seem real. The support I've got from my fans, from friends and family, and the people around me at my management company, 19 Entertainment, and at the record company has been incredible.

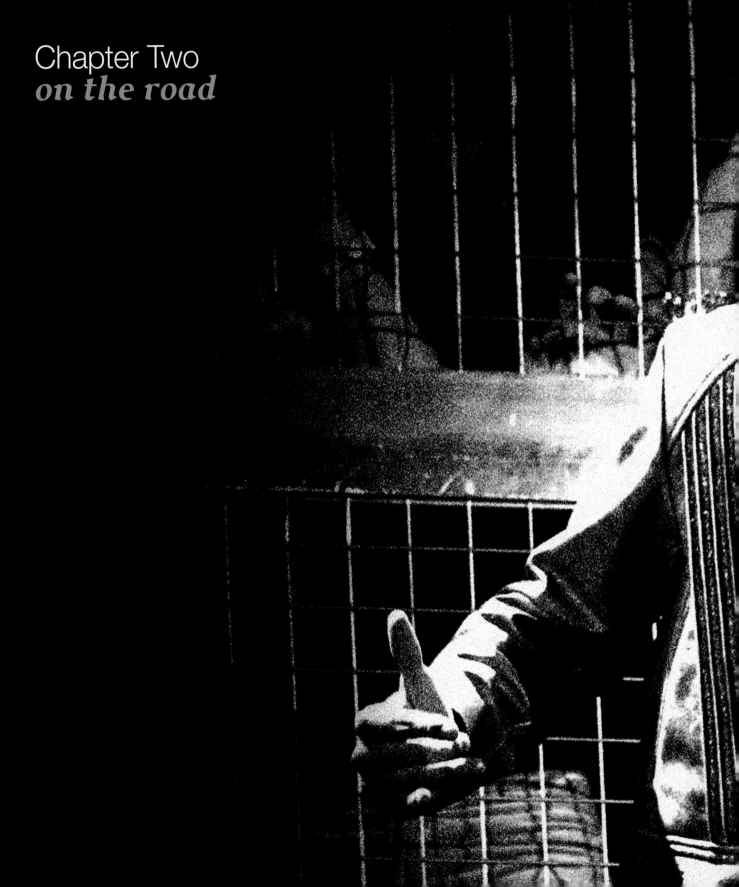

Chapter Two
on the road

'On the last tour
there were **loads of
clever things we did,**
like showing me
texting the crowd
on the **big screen**'

Gareth is sitting on one of two sofas in his manager Simon Fuller's office. In between the sofas, exotic fresh flowers decorate a low table, which sits on the deepest, softest rug you've ever seen. The office's state-of-the-art audio and video equipment is all switched off and there is an overall feeling of peace. Gareth's got a stinking cold, but he's in a good mood, and while I'm fiddling with the tape recorder he's happy to sign photos for his fan club and a good luck card for a friend's daughter who's in the middle of her GCSEs. Once settled Gareth starts talking about the tour…

The tour that Will, Zoë and I did was an awesome experience. It came quite quickly after the *Pop Idol* tour that all ten finalists did together, so I was a bit worried that no one would want to come and see us! I needn't have worried at all – everywhere we went the crowds were huge. We played fantastic venues including London Arena, Wembley Arena, Sheffield Arena, Newcastle Telewest Arena, Nottingham Arena, Manchester Evening News Arena, Birmingham NEC and Glasgow SECC. It was a huge show with pyrotechnics, a proper band, a stage that went right out into the middle of the crowd and loads and loads of amazing lights. We even had girls dancing in cages on the stage. I think they were supposed to be competition winners in each town, but I'm sure one or two of them came everywhere with us … anyway, it was cheaper than getting proper dancers!

If you were one of the people who came to the show, then I hope you enjoyed it. The people that the audience sees on stage every night are just the tip of the iceberg. On tour there's a whole army of people that are with you to make sure that everything happens. Everything's covered. Drivers, set builders, lighting, sound, security, wardrobe, hair and make-up, the band, backing

singers, dancers, tour managers, personal assistants and us! The team we had was excellent. When I go out on tour on my own, I want to take some of the same people with me. It's important for me to build a team that I want to be around me for the rest of my career, like a personal assistant, hair and make-up; people who'll support me.

Sometimes on a tour the artists tend to stay out of the way and not get matey with the crew, but I like to get involved in everything. You make a lot of friends that way. It's especially useful to have a friend in 'artist catering' so that there'll always be something on the menu that I like.

We travelled between venues on this really cool double-decker tour bus. It had ten or twelve bunks upstairs, a kitchen area with a microwave, a DVD player, and a video – even a PlayStation. Obviously the whole tour entourage didn't fit on one bus. Our bus was just Will, Zoë and me, our personal assistants, the tour manager and some security people. I made sure I had first choice of the bunks.

I set up a little recording studio in one of the bunks because I was starting to write stuff for the second album. I had my laptop and my keyboard and some little speakers. We were driving along and I'd be bouncing up and down, trying to play bits on the keyboard. It's lucky I don't get travel sick.

When we arrive in a city, we all check into our hotels. The artists stay in one hotel and most of the crew stay in a different hotel. We stayed in some top hotels and most of the time we got the best rooms, the suites. There was one time that we complained. When we went to Birmingham I'd checked in, and I was sitting in my room looking around, and I thought to myself, 'It's just not very nice.' Then my room phone went and it was Will. He said, 'These rooms aren't very nice are they?' I agreed, so we went down and asked if we could move. That's typical me. I had to wait until someone else didn't like them before doing anything about it! I do have to say that the rooms they moved us to were lovely.

If I'm able to save some money, I will do. On the tour there are free meals every day in catering. Technically it's not free because eventually I'll have to pay for it out of album sales or whatever, but at the time it feels like it's free. I'd always eat backstage. Every day I'd take loads of cans from catering, put them in my bag and use the mini-bar at the hotel to keep them cool. That way I didn't spend so much on room service. Prices in hotels can be just stupid.

'The people that the audience sees on stage every night are just the tip of the iceberg'

There were some really late nights on the tour. Really late. Some nights we were up until five or six in the morning just having a laugh and being stupid. You can't be that late every night though, because you have to be able to perform the next day.

When we were in Manchester we decided we wanted a night out, so a party was arranged in a club. It was well cool. Normally, though, we were just in the hotel bar or in someone's suite. A couple of times I've bought drinks for the whole bar, but then you get complete strangers going, 'Yeah, I'll have one!' You can't do that every night either; you'd end up broke.

Having said all that, I've never woken up and thought, 'I can't do this today.' I'm really good with being tired and still performing. I've trained myself to power nap. I can sleep anywhere, and I mean anywhere. Even if I've got twenty minutes between meetings, I can just drop off and catch up on my sleep. If I didn't do that I'd never be able to cope with my schedule.

What made it more tiring for me was the fact that I was promoting 'The Long And Winding Road'/'Suspicious Minds' at the time. Some days I was up and down the country like a yo-yo. When everyone else on the tour was going from city to city, I'd be up at the crack of dawn, down to London to do a TV show or something, then back up to wherever they were just in time to go on stage. It was madness.

I didn't sleep in my own hotel room every night. Sometimes Mum and Dad would come to see me and they'd take over my suite. I'd have to call Zoë up and ask if I could stop with her in her room. We'd stay up all night messing around, just chatting. She's such a laugh.

'I can sleep anywhere, *and I mean anywhere'*

There was no love action for me on the tour, which is a bit sad really, what with all those fancy hotel rooms. I didn't get any bootie calls on the room phones! But there was a lot of flirting going on at the parties. You know what it's like: talking, maybe some dancing. I couldn't really do anything because there were always journalists in the hotels. The temptation is always there, because you're there and you have loads of girls near you who are just ready. You have to tell yourself, 'Whoa, steady on!' Without my sister there, keeping the girls away, I have to be my own minder – and that's dangerous. I do trust myself, though.

Another incredible thing about touring and staying in hotels is that the fans always find out where I'm staying, most of the time before I do. Sometimes they book into the hotels, or they wait outside, even if it's raining. It would be nice to be able to invite them all in, but that would be mad. We're not the only people

staying at the hotel, and it would disturb the other guests, who would be a bit annoyed if we invited loads of people in. Instead I'll sit and chat to them. They don't get invited up to the room, but I do like to chat to them.

When we were Holland it was raining the worst I've ever seen. These two Dutch girls slept outside the venue just so they'd be able to see me. You should have seen them, they were proper soaked and their sleeping bags were like swimming pools. They were only about sixteen.

The best bit about touring has to be the actual show. The crowds, the lights, the noise – that's what it's all about, it's what I'd always dreamed of doing. When I'm on stage I wear this 'bug' thing in my ear that lets me hear the music and my voice. Without it, I wouldn't be able to tell which song the band are playing, because the crowd is so loud it's unbelievable. I hold the record for the loudest scream – well, my crowd do, not me!

'Every day I'd take loads of cans from catering, put them in my bag and use the mini-bar at the hotel to keep them cool'

'I hold the record for the loudest scream – well, my crowd do, not me!'

The sound guys on the tour worked with The Beatles, ages and ages ago, so they know about everything. When Will and I were doing the last bit, when we walk out on to the stage in the middle of the crowd, we're completely surrounded by fans – it's so hard to hear. It's hard for the sound guys. We're on stage, looking at the sound guys, pointing up, which means, 'Can you turn up the volume in the earpiece so we can hear?' The sound guys are just shrugging because it's already at full volume. It's crazy. They told us they'd never heard anything as loud since the hysteria that used to happen when The Beatles performed. It was a massive thrill to hear that, a real plus.

I love all that though. I like looking out for cool banners. If they're miles away, I can't see them. Without the house lights on, you can only see about the first ten rows, and after that you can see those glowsticks and flashing things that people have, but if people near the front have banners then I'll definitely read them. On the *Pop Idol* tour when all ten of us were on stage for the finale there was a massive banner that said, 'GARETH FANCY A SHAG?' in huge letters. We all saw it and all ten of us were laughing our heads off. It was so funny. Is that approach going to work? Put it this way, it's always nice to be noticed! I do like to flirt with the audience. I try and flirt with everyone in the whole venue! I try and make everyone in the crowd think, 'Oooh, yeah, he's looking at me!' They should think that, because I am.

One thing I want to try and do when I tour on my own is talk to the crowd between songs. On the last tour there were loads of clever things we did, like showing me texting the crowd on the big screen, or holding up cards with stuff I wanted to say. I want to be able to be spontaneous with the crowd, react to things they're shouting, you know? They all know I've got a stammer, so there's not really any pressure on me.

The tour went really smoothly apart from one of the Newcastle shows. I nearly died in Newcastle! I had a near-death experience. The stage had two huge scaffolding towers, one on each side, with steps that lead up to a platform. On my first song, the Michael Jackson one, 'The Way You Make Me Feel', I ran across the stage, up the steps and go to the edge of the platform to get as near as I could to the crowd at the sides. Because it's my first song, I was right into it, with my adrenalin pumping and the crowd going mad. Anyway, around these platforms were two safety bars, one about chest high and one about thigh high. There was also a kind of panel, like a skirting board, that stops your feet from going over the edge. It's very safe.

Except for this one show in Newcastle. I was full into it, you know, bouncing across the stage, 'The way you make-ah me feel...' and I go running up the steps of this tower, '... you really

'The tour went really smoothly apart from one of the Newcastle shows. I nearly died in Newcastle!'

'On a tour it's kind of a tradition to play jokes on the artists on the last night'

turn me o-on...' I got to the platform and moved towards the edge and I skidded. Usually the panel would stop my foot from going over the edge but, that night, for some reason, it wasn't there. My feet went right off the edge and I slipped under the safety bars. The microphone was in my right hand so I reached out with my left hand and luckily managed to grab one of the safety bars. I looked down and I could see that I was right over the guitar tech area. Thirty feet below me there were loads of guitars pointing up at me like jagged rocks. I remember thinking, 'If I fall now, I'll be wrecked.' I would at least have broken my back. The stupid part was that all this time I kept on singing! There I am, thirty feet up, and I'm still singing '...you knock me off-ah my fe-eeet...' I think the crowd thought it was part of the act. They didn't seem worried, they just kept on cheering. They did all go 'ooooooh' at one point, but I think they thought I did it every night. I managed to pull myself back onto the platform with my left hand and carry on with the show, but it was proper scary. Put it this way, I made sure the panel was there every night after that.

On a tour it's kind of a tradition to play jokes on the artists on the last night. For one song the piano wasn't working. They brought it out on to the stage and it wouldn't work. So there was me, sat there, nothing. For ages I was saying, 'What's happening with this piano?' I had to start the song without any music. I'm still not sure whether that was a joke or just a dodgy piano.

There was one thing that definitely was a joke. If you went to the show, you'll remember the bit every night where I pretend to argue with the guitarist about what song we're going to do. Well on the last night, we started arguing like normal, and the whole band just walked off stage! I was like, 'What am I gonna do?' It was hard for me, because of my speech, I couldn't just tell the crowd what was happening, so I was just stood there for about five minutes. If you've never stood in front of a big crowd doing absolutely nothing, then let me tell you, five minutes is a long time. The crowd went quiet for a bit when they realised something was up, then they started chanting 'Gareth, Gareth, Gareth'. Eventually I managed get it together enough to beg the band, 'Please come back. Pleeeeease.'

To get them back for that, in the last song, the Elvis number, I went round the whole band one by one with the microphone and made them all sing. They hated that!

I can't wait to tour on my own and hopefully something will happen in 2004, and hopefully you'll be there. Yes, you, reading the book – I mean you! See you there!

Chapter Three
family, friends and girlfriends

The best thing I've been able to do since I've become famous is buy a house. It's not for me, but for my family. It's up north with a couple of acres of land. It's just on the outskirts of Bradford and it's amazing, out in the fields, surrounded by real countryside.

It's also an investment. I never take anything for granted, which is why I'm investing in property, stocks and shares. My dad helps me with that. I don't fully understand about finances, so Dad helps me out. I never got into what I do because I wanted to be rich, but because I love music, and I love singing. Hopefully that always comes across.

It takes ages to notice you're making money. The public think I've got millions and millions already. I haven't – yet!

I remember, before I was famous, I used to buy small presents for my mum and dad and my sisters at Christmas. Dad used to get socks or boxers, mum used to get cheap perfume. In total I'd spend about £80 on the whole family. Now they get bigger presents like phones or nice clothes. I don't get them all cars or anything! They don't have to get me bigger presents, though I did get a really cool hi-fi system from them last Christmas.

I've been really lucky with the parents I have. You hear horror stories about parents who push and push, parents who just wanted to be famous themselves. My parents aren't like that at all. They just encouraged us to fulfil our dreams, they wanted us to do whatever was in our hearts. I'll never be able to pay them back for all the things they've done for me.

They worked hard at what they did, the money that they got they invested it into our lives. Music lessons are expensive but they'd go without stuff so we could keep going.

When they knew that I really wanted to be a pop star they even paid for us to go and record some songs in a proper recording studio. It was a lot of money but we got a whole day in a studio. Me and my sister Nicola recorded a duet and some cover versions to send off to record companies. We also went to a photographic studio as well to have a picture taken for the front cover. I was wearing jeans and a T-shirt, the white suit didn't come in till later! The pictures still exist: they're absolutely terrible!

'I never got into what I do because I wanted to be rich, but because I love music'

As you probably know, there are only ten and a half months between Nicola and me. We could have been in the same year at school, which would have been weird, but because our birthdays fell when they did, she was in the year below me. We still hang around together now. Even though she's my little sister, she's so protective of me. She'd never encourage me to chat up a girl, ever. Even if I'm just talking to a girl she just hates it. She stops me from getting into situations I shouldn't, but I do have to tell her back off sometimes. How do I stop her? I just slap her! Only joking, I love Nicola! We're still best mates now, I mean how many boys my age would choose to go on holiday with their sister unless all her fit mates were going as well? Nicola has got such an amazing voice. It won't be long until she's up there at the top, you know.

Me and my sister have the same friends, there's a group of about five or six of us that hang out together. My friends all do normal jobs or they're at university. Sometimes I regret not going to uni, but I wouldn't swap what I'm doing for anything. One time they were all staying in my flat while I was recording. The night before I was due in the studio we all went out, had a drink or two, then crashed out at my place. I got up first, and got picked up and driven to the studio. When I got there the producer said we needed to get some crowd style backing vocals, you know, 'Whoa, wahey', that kind of thing. I said my friends and my sister are down, we can get them all in to do that! So I called home, got them up, and soon there were five of us crammed into a vocal booth about the size of a phone booth. We were all just having a laugh with the waheys and whoas, just being stupid really, but the producer liked it and now my mates are on the record! That's really nice for me. Save money, get your friends in!

'Sometimes I regret not going to uni'

GIRLS

Of course I do find some of the girls that approach me attractive. I've had a couple of things with people, never anything serious. We'd meet, go for dinner or whatever, but so far I've never thought, 'This is the one'. No one's been introduced to Mum and Dad yet. It would have to be really serious for that to happen, and besides, they'd have to get past Nicola first! I think when that does happen, it's not something I'd want to talk about a lot. I think relationships with people should be private – between the two of you. Who wants to know about them?

I read this story in the press that said I'd been 'advised' by my record company that I couldn't have a girlfriend for five years, which is absolutely rubbish.

When I look for a girl I haven't got a preference on things like hair colour, but I am going to try and get the best I can get.

I know I don't sound very fussy, but I am. The personality is very important to me. Because of my speech they'd have to be patient with me. They'd have to be able to read! Because I'd be writing loads of things down.

To a certain extent, she'd have to share my religious beliefs, as I wouldn't want her doing anything that I am against. But, at the same time I wouldn't say to a girl you've got to believe this to go out with me.

I couldn't imagine going out with a celebrity like Britney Spears. Not because she'd get loads of attention from guys, the same kind of attention that I get from girls – I wouldn't be bothered by that at all. If the guys were just looking at her, then that'd be fine. You can look but you can't touch! The difficult thing would be never seeing her. She'd be going round the world all the time like I do, her schedule would be ridiculous, and we'd only have to rearrange everything just to be in the same country for a couple of days.

I'm very demanding, I think. Demanding on someone's time. I'd want them to be with me every second of the day. Even though my job takes me all over the place, I'd want them with me. If we did have to be apart I'd be on the phone all the time. It is possible to have a serious girlfriend at this stage in my career, but it's really hard. I haven't got much time to go looking, which is a shame. When I was younger I had girlfriends all the time. I've always liked having someone special to do things with, spend time with.

There is someone that I'm very close to now. We go out sometimes, we have fun, go for dinner, that kind of thing. It's not a secret, but equally I don't really talk about it. It works better to keep it private, and she feels the same.

Chapter Four
celebrity

I suppose I am a celebrity, but I don't think I'm any different from how I've always been. I'm still the same person with the same friends, the same faults and the same sense of humour.

I've got used to seeing pictures of myself in the press looking a right state. A lot of the pictures of me that turn up in the papers make me laugh. There's usually a sensible explanation behind them, even if sometimes I look like I'm really out of it. It's like when you get your holiday pictures back and there are loads where you look awful. You'll show your mates most of them anyway, but there's usually one or two that 'go missing' before you show everyone. They're the pictures that get printed!

There was this one picture that was described as 'Gareth Gates, the singer, leaning against a lamppost getting his wallet out after a night at the Met Bar.' I've never been to the Met Bar in my life. Never! I was really sober in that picture. (Well not as bad as I looked!) In the picture it said I was supposed to be leaning against the lamppost – well, I'm not leaning, I'm just standing there with a lamppost behind me! Mind you, I did look as if I was chatting up the lamppost!

What happened was that I was in a taxi when I asked the driver to stop at a cashpoint, because I didn't have any cash on me. He pulled in at this cashpoint, I jumped out with my wallet in my hand and there's a paparazzi photographer there, snapping away with a flash. I instinctively turned away so in the photo I looked like I was stumbling. I jumped straight back into the cab and we drove off and he took me to another cashpoint to get the money out. It's as simple as that. But the photo had been taken and whoever saw it would think I'd been wandering around drunk, leaning on lampposts and waving my wallet around like a fool!

Having said all that, I did look a bit worse for wear in the picture. I can see why people would think that. The trouble is, I could probably explain away every dodgy paparazzi picture, but it would take forever. You just have to live with it.

I didn't mind when pictures of Nicola and me on holiday turned up in the newspapers. They were nice enough photos and we were behaving ourselves in them. We didn't look stupid. That's one of the reasons I went on holiday with Nicola. I've never been on a big lads' holiday. I have been to Ibiza and Majorca on holiday when I was younger, but not on a mad clubbing holiday. It wouldn't be possible for me to go on a lads' holiday now. A few of my mates would be up for a boozy time and would definitely be chasing the women, but if I was there it would be a problem. The press would be after me – they'd have a field day. I don't think I'm missing out by not being able to go on one of those holidays, though. I'm the sort of person who doesn't really have regrets.

Recently I was in Amsterdam and I went out for a few drinks. I'm huge in Holland now, I was number one there for three weeks, but they got shots of me looking really stupid. Because it was in the heart of Amsterdam, near the red-light district, they said that I'd been to a bondage club. I thought, 'What do they think they're writing?' It was all wrong, but you just have to get on with it really. It's frustrating but as long as I know what I actually did, that's what counts. As long as I know the truth, and the people around me know the truth. It's not all bad with the papers, though. They print loads of good stuff about me too. It must be hard sometimes just filling up the pages every single day. I'd be more worried if I wasn't in there at all!

The whole time I've been a celebrity I've probably been to about two or three proper showbiz parties and I'm not rushing to go to any more. Those parties are quite false. There are a lot of people just going 'mwah, mwah', you know, air-kissing. I don't do that air-kissing thing. I do a proper kiss on the cheek. Maybe both cheeks if they're lucky. If they air-kiss me, I just think, 'What are you doing?'

I'm myself all the time, I haven't got a party mode. If I want to talk to someone, I'll talk to them; if I don't, I won't. I'm always friendly, though. I don't like being rude. A lot of people imagine that London is full of celebrities, constantly hanging out with each other, but it's just not like that. In all honesty, I haven't really had the time to make many friends. It's hard. Especially when you get famous the way that I did. I was thrown

'I could probably explain away every dodgy paparazzi picture, but it would take forever. You just have to live with it'

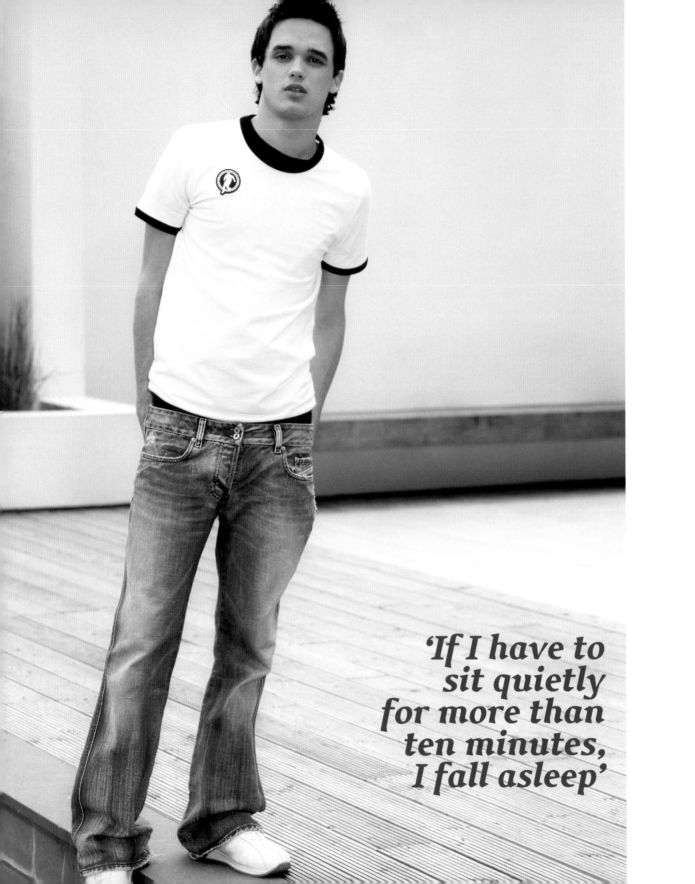

'If I have to
sit quietly
for more than
ten minutes,
I fall asleep'

straight into celebrity. I didn't have to go to all the parties to get myself known. I was known by the whole country instantly. I missed out on that whole getting to know people, that bonding time. It's a shame, because sometimes I see other stars at roadshows and things and they're all having a laugh with each other because they know each other. I miss out on that. I'm not sad in any way though, because I've got really good friends that I've known for years.

I know for a fact that there are stars who don't like me because of the way I made it. I would absolutely love to name names, but I'm not going to. Some of these stars who don't like the way I made it can't even sing. How can you turn round and say something about me when you can't even sing? A lot of other stars did all their auditions and trials behind closed doors, whereas on *Pop Idol* it was all in the public eye. If you had a bad day on *Pop Idol*, you were out of the competition, so you had to be good all the time. And you had to be able to sing, it wasn't just on your image or stuff like that. When I started out that was one of the things that really annoyed me. Not everyone is like that though. The most famous person I've met is George Michael and he was lovely, and he's incredibly talented. Westlife are nice lads too; they're a real laugh.

There are stars that I wish I'd never met, because the way that you see them from the outside, is, 'Oh, they're absolutely amazing, they're really cool', but if you get to know them, get to see what happens around them, you realise that they're not quite as they seem. Their attitude towards the performance, to the fans, can be appalling. If I ever start going that way, I want someone to tell me. I never ever want to be like that. I'm the same person you see on and off screen.

I do enjoy doing TV shows though. There's always a real buzz before you go to do your bit, and, no matter how many times I've been on TV, there's always that feeling that something could go wrong! The people behind the scenes at TV shows are really helpful. If it's a live show it can look like chaos but everyone has got their own jobs to do, and they're all really good at their jobs which helps me relax. There's always stuff to do, like make-up, getting dressed, sometimes there are interviews to do, and there are always people who want an autograph. I'd much rather have people

to talk to and muck around with, rather than just sit there and wait to be called. If I have to sit quietly for more than ten minutes, I drop off to sleep.

Something else about celebrities: they're nearly always smaller in real life. Some stars are really tiny. Another thing is with female stars, the ones that look absolutely amazing in pictures usually aren't so amazing in real life, but the ones who look OK in pictures can be amazing.

'Celebrities are nearly always smaller in real life'

celebrity
– a few questions

Do you push to the front in queues?

Usually when I'm in a restaurant or in a cinema, I don't want anyone to know I'm there, so I'll do what everyone else does and queue. I wear my cap out, and a big coat. In the summer I'll be so hot, I'll be dripping! I try not to get noticed. People do spot me and point at me and whisper, 'It's him, it's him! He's really sweaty!'

Have you ever not signed an autograph?

Never. Well, no. If I'm able to I will. But if I have to get some-where really, really quickly, I just have to say no. It's hard for me, because I like signing autographs and talking to fans. I have to say sorry. I never got anyone's autograph when I was little.

Do you get loads of free stuff now you're famous?

I get a few things, yeah, but it's not like tons and tons of stuff. It's not things like cars and houses; it's more like hair gel. I don't need hair gel!

Do you get into places where no one else can go?

Yeah, sometimes. If there's something I really want or somewhere I really want to go I'll let someone know. If they don't sort it out I'll throw a strop, 'That's it, I'm off, I'm leaving!' Only joking – I just ask them to try their best. I'm an easy person to work with. My team would tell you that I'm the nicest person they've worked with.

Would you ever use your fame to try and pull?

Er, yes, I have done. Mmmm. Yes, definitely. More often, though, I've set my mates up with people. Not famous people. I'll be in a bar with my mates and a girl will come up to me and we'll get talking. My mates will be like, 'She's gorgeous'. So I say, 'This is my mate so and so.' Then I say I'm just nipping to the loo or something and leave them to it. But, for me that's nice.

It must be cool being one of your mates then? They get to be on the record, and you set them up with fit girls, they see you on tour and stuff. How can someone apply to become a 'mate of Gareth'?

It would be wicked! I should advertise.

Chapter Five
my fans

'One **pair of knickers** had a **message sewn on in sequins!**'

My fans are amazing. On tour they were just the best. I tell you something, there are some good-looking fans when I'm on stage. The one thing I bet the people don't realise is that I'm just as excited about being there as they are! I know it sounds corny but my fans really do mean loads to me. Considering that I wasn't able to talk to them when they came to see me on tour, or that I didn't do all the school tours and stuff that most other people in my position did, it's brilliant to have such loyal support. I'll never take that for granted.

Since the launch of my official fan club in July 2002, thousands of members have joined, and there are still hundreds joining every week. Every day a sack-full of photos, letters, cards and presents arrives. People go through everything for me and make sure that when I pop in to visit, I get to see everything that's been sent in. Since the start it feels like the presents I get sent have got a bit older. I'm getting fewer cuddly toys and more clothes and aftershave. Some people even send presents in for my family.

I get sent underwear in the post. Boys' and girls' underwear. I guess the boys' stuff is for me to wear; I hope the girls' stuff isn't! Sometimes the underwear will have messages written on it – one pair of knickers

had a message sewn on in sequins! I've been sent loads of marriage proposals. Some fans have even 'married' me online, and have sent me the marriage certificates to prove it! Once when I was online I said I'd like a baby grand piano, and a load of the fan club members got together on one of the message boards and decided that they'd all send a little bit of money in and get the fan club to go and buy me one. I do love all the presents, but please don't anyone spend a fortune on me – a nice card or a letter is every bit as nice a present.

Since the fan club was launched there have been three times when their office was swamped with cards. First up was my birthday, which, for those of you who don't know, is (hint, hint!) 12 July. It was incredible. Two sacks full of cards arrived and the fan club had only been going for eleven days.

At Christmas five sacks of cards and presents arrived. I got loads of cards with hedgehogs on, and loads of toy hedgehogs, because of the way my hair was. That wasn't the worst though, because when Valentine's Day came it went loopy. It looked like a Clinton Card shop: there were big padded cards, teddy bears, roses, love poems, letters, it was mad!

I like to go on the official website to read the message board as often as I can, because it's the best way to find out what my fans are talking about. They're really honest. If I've had to rush off at a concert, or if I've worn a dodgy shirt on TV, it's always on the message board. The fans seem to know stuff about what I'm doing before I do! I've done webchats every couple of months since the site has launched and when people start realising that I'm online, and that I'm answering people's questions, the message boards go manic, with hundreds of fans asking questions all at once. 'What are you wearing?' 'Would you ever go out with a fan?' 'Would you ever go out with meeeeeeeeee!!!!!!!!' That kind of thing! As well as the official website, someone told me that there are hundreds of unofficial Gareth websites that fans have set up on the internet themselves. I have looked at quite a few of the fan sites and I have to say the standard is pretty amazing. I don't know where they get all the information, but even I learned stuff about me on them. Apparently there's an 'I Hate Gareth' site! I won't be visiting that one, then.

It's not just the fans who join the fan club who are excellent though. When I meet people at concerts, or at TV shows, everyone is really nice to me. Because *Pop Idol* was so big, it's not just teenagers who ask to talk to me, it's grannies. Grannies always ask for autographs, and they always say it's for someone else. Sometimes girls will hand me something to sign and when I look at what they've put in my hand it's their phone number!

The only time it's ever a hassle is when I'm out with mates, and that's just because it's not really fans who come and talk, it's lads who have had a few drinks and they're showing off. Sometimes it's girls who come over and chat, and I can see their boyfriends over the other side of the pub, and I'm thinking, 'What's going on here?' But most of the time it's cool. I don't go out to be the big star or anything and I think people can tell that and treat me well.

Alexandra Jones
www.garethofficialfanclub.com

Gareth's great. He's a genuinely lovely guy who's currently living his dream of being a pop star. In this situation he could have let it all go to his head and become full of himself, but he hasn't at all – he's still a Bradford lad but with more women after him! He's incredibly mischievous when we're filming and he's always mucking around when he visits the fan club. His fans mean a lot to him and even though he's busy and his schedule frequently takes him out of the country, he still makes a huge effort to keep in contact with his fans via the fan club.

PopIdol
Tour 2002
featuring the BIG BLUE

GarethGates
What My Heart Wants To Say

LIMITED EDITION CD2 INCLUDES: PREVIOUSLY UNRELEASED SONG, EXCLUSIVE BEHIND THE SCENES FOOTAGE + GARETH POSTER

GarethGates
Anyone Of Us (Stupid Mistake)

features a brand new track, fantastic video and exclusive footage

CD1 INCLUDES: BRAND NEW SONG + THE AMAZING VIDEO

GARETH GATES

GarethGates

GarethGates
OFFICIAL MAGAZINE COLLECTION

charity begins at home

I was really excited about doing Comic Relief because, right from the beginning of my career, I said that I wanted to help people and this was an opportunity to fulfil that dream. It was first mentioned sometime in December 2002, but it was at the Record of the Year show that I found out the song was going to be 'Spirit In The Sky'. At first I was thinking, 'Oh crap.'

Then I went away over New Year to the Maldives then to Dubai with my sister. I was getting calls on holiday about doing 'Spirit'. I was saying, 'But I don't know if I like it.' Then they told me that the Kumars were involved and I changed my mind straight away. I had watched the Kumars before, not every show, but enough to know who they were and how funny they are. Whatever song we were doing, they were bound to make it hilarious, and people would see it was a bit of fun rather than a serious track.

We didn't record the song together. First the track was all laid out: music, backing vocals and so on, and then they went into the studio to do their bits. After they'd finished, I went in and did my vocal. I was in and out in a day. It's actually a really, really easy song to do. Normally I do a lot of my own backing vocals but I didn't have to do that this time because most of the backing vocals were female. The first time I actually met the Kumars was when we shot the video.

That was one long, long day. Without the Kumars being there, no one would have been able to do it. They were making us all laugh. It was really, really cool. They stay in character as the Kumars when they're dressed up. That old lady is really a much younger woman, the comedian Meera Syal, and she was getting quite frisky. And when I saw the dancers I was like, 'Wa-hey!' They're probably the sauciest dancers I've worked with. Saucy Indian dancers! You know the way that they made my hair look first thing in the morning when I'm in the pyjamas? That's exactly what it looks like first thing in the morning!

When we performed 'Spirit' on TV shows with all the smoke and the dancers in front of each other it was really funny to do. The whole campaign was just about having a laugh, there was no element of being serious at all. I didn't feel any pressure that it wouldn't sell, because I know how much people care about supporting Comic Relief. It went to number one and loads of money was raised for some really good causes. I'd like to take this chance to thank everyone who bought it, or supported Comic Relief in other ways. You did a good thing! Do I like the song any more now? Hmmmm … Of course! I absolutely love it!

'That's exactly how my hair looks first thing in the morning!'

'They're probably
the sauciest dancers
I've worked with'

I used to watch Comic Relief when I was growing up, it's one of those things that the whole family used to watch together. I didn't always give money though, which I feel a bit guilty about. I did give money this year. If Comic Relief asked me to be involved again, I'd jump at the chance. Whatever they asked me to do, it's great to be able to help.

Helping people is not just about money, it's about giving your time as well. A lot of charities approach me to do stuff, but there's only a certain amount I can do. Through Comic Relief I've become involved with a charity called Body and Soul, which supports people affected by HIV and AIDS. Another charity I support is Robyn Brooks' Appeal – Robyn is a little girl who is terminally ill. She lives in Rochdale and her family is a friend of my family. She's only six years old. There's a website where you can find out more about her – www.robynbrooks.co.uk.

What I do if a children's charity calls up, or an HIV charity, is to tell them about the charities I already support and say, 'I'm helping this charity – if you help this charity as well, then we'll all be helping each other.'

There's one other charity that I'm heavily involved with and that's the Restoration Trust. It's part of my church in Bradford, the Abundant Life Church, and they help out people there, the homeless and the hungry. This is something that I've been involved in for ages. I believe that we're here to help people less fortunate than ourselves. In my position I'm able to help people. If I wasn't helping, then it would be wrong.

Bradford is still where my heart is. There are terrible things happening all over the world, and you should never forget what's happening out there, but there are things much closer to home that have to be changed. To me, helping people is really important. There are things you can do on your own doorstep.

My relationship with the church has stayed constant throughout everything that's happened to me. They don't treat me any differently now I'm a celebrity. There's no posters of me outside the church saying, 'Now starring Gareth Gates', no pictures of me with my arm round Jesus!

'Helping people is really important. There are things you can do on your own doorstep'

I'm on a lot of our church albums as a backing vocalist but I don't know if the sales have picked up since I became famous! I am on the covers, but there are loads of other people and I'm really small. Because I'd only go to my own church in Bradford, I don't get to go as often as I'd like. If I do get time off on a Sunday, I'll go up north for the day, go home and go to church. To do that, I have to leave my London flat about 5 a.m. I get driven up there, but my personal assistant doesn't have to come with me, that would be a bit harsh! I get there about 8.30, see my mum and dad and my sisters, they're like, 'Gar-eth, it's so early!' I'm like, 'Early? Get up!'

I have a cup of tea there and Mum will make me some breakfast, then at 9.30 I get ready for church. My church is really cool and modern, so when we get dressed in our Sunday best we don't get all suited up, but we put our trendiest gear on. There are loads of young people there who all dress up so I've got to look even better than them – which is hard to top, because they're well smart. I have to wear stuff you can only get in London!

There's loads of singing at church and I always join in with all that. There are about 1,500 people in the church – it's massive. There are some amazing, amazing musicians at that church. If I ever needed a choir on one of my records, they'd be awesome.

It's not necessarily a cool thing to be part of a church in this country but it's part of me, no matter what people think. I couldn't care less if people say stuff about me going to church. I've never had big arguments with anyone about it because it's not an issue that I'd argue about. Believe what you want to believe and I'll believe what I want to believe. It's much more common for American artists to talk about religion. You always hear American artists thanking God at awards ceremonies and on their album sleeves, but I'm not sure everyone actually believes that there is a God, they just say it. I think, 'What are you doing, you idiots?' Some people say it to be safe, like a superstitious thing. You know, I'd better thank Him just in case. They might be genuine believers, but I think the majority of people just say it. If I won a big award I probably wouldn't be able to thank God in my speech. I probably wouldn't be able to say anything! I could always hold a sign up saying, 'Thanks God'.

The church will carry on being part of my life forever. You get some stars who aren't religious when they're younger turning to religion later in life, to Buddhism or whatever. I'm lucky; this is something I've already got within me. All my friends are part of the church in Bradford, it's the place where all the people that I care about most are. These are the same friends who come down and crash at my house, go out on the town with me, come into the recording studio with me. People have this image of church-goers as people who don't go out, don't drink, don't have a laugh – that's just absolute rubbish. We're normal people.

'Helping people is not just about money, it's about giving your time as well'

Charlotte Hickson, 19 Entertainment
The excitement of working with Gareth, who had dreamed of being a pop star from a very young age, and being able to help him live his dream, has been fantastic.

Working with Gareth is different from working with any other artist, due to the difficulties he has with his speech. For him to have been so successful so quickly is testament to his musical ability and his dedication to the job. With him not being able to communicate with his fans in the traditional way through TV interviews and so on, maintaining this success is another achievement in itself.

When Simon Fuller signed Gareth, we knew that we would have a lot of fun ahead of us. He is extremely hard working, very funny and appreciates the position he is in.

Sonny Takhar, General Manager of S Records
Most people who become famous because of a reality TV show only ever sell records in the country where the show is screened. Gareth is unique in that he's come from that genre and become a global star. That's because he's a great singer, a talented song-writer and has genuine star quality. There's a real aura about him.

Dave Shack, Director of International, BMG Records
The reaction the rest of the world has had to Gareth has been unlike anything I've ever seen before. He's been top of the charts in countries he's never even visited. No matter where he goes, the reaction is always the same. Obviously the records do a lot of the work, but an artist still has to win people over on a personal level. Gareth is always on form: no matter how tired he is, he can step off a long flight and be charming, sexy and professional straight away. He's a pleasure to work with. The aim now is to consolidate all the work Gareth has done in all the different territories.

I've done a lot of travelling since it all started. Norway, Sweden, Germany, Spain, Holland, America, Belgium, Italy, France, Scotland, Ireland, Wales and I'm sure there's other places that I've missed out!

Since January 2003 I've been away all the time doing promotion for the last album and recording the new one so I'm probably only in the country two days a week. I've had to get used to living away from home, I'm always packing and unpacking suitcases – I'm an expert packer now. When I go away I take loads and loads of clothes, loads of shoes, loads of stuff. I know it sounds more like a girl going on holiday, but if I'm doing promotional work I have to carry all the clothes that I might need. If I'm recording it's not so much hassle, just a few T-shirts, jeans and a couple of warm tops – it can get proper cold in Scandinavia.

'I am always on the phone to the people I love'

There are certain things that I have to have with me wherever I go. I always carry my wallet, even if there's no money in it. If I'm on a work trip I don't pay for much. If we're out and there's someone from the record company or my management there, they'll pay. I suppose sometimes I could go, 'Don't worry, I'll take care of that', but it all comes out of the same pot eventually.

I've got an iPod so I can take all my favourite records everywhere with me. iPods are so cool. You can get thousands of songs on them. I always take my writing book, which I fill with pages and pages of thoughts and ideas for songs. I don't keep a diary, but my dad keeps telling me I should. He says it's important because in the future it'll help me remember what really happened, otherwise all I'll have to go on is newspaper cuttings. I'm not one of those people who takes photos of my family everywhere with them, but I am always on the phone to the people I love.

The stammer can be a problem on the phone, but people that I know really well, like my close friends or my family, obviously know all about it and we can just have a normal conversation. If it's an important phone call, or I've got to speak to a journalist or something, then it is hard, I do struggle. I send a lot of text messages. Text messaging is a real gift for me because without it I'd be on the phone for hours and hours! If I'm trying to meet up with one of my mates and I need to tell them where to meet and what time, it can take me hours to say, and I mean hours, so I'll just stop the conversation, say I'll text whoever it is the details and hang up.

My phone bills are stupid. I get them sent to my management now, and I've just opened one. It's over £800 – for one month! I know I make a lot of calls from abroad, but that's sky high. It adds up to about £10,000 a year. It's crazy, isn't it?

When I go to countries where I haven't been before, the journalists ask all sorts of questions like, 'What's your name?' Er, it's me! Strange to ask me what my name is, you think they'd do their research! They ask my age, stuff about my mum and dad, have you got any brothers and sisters and they always ask me where I'm from. I learnt pretty quickly that most people outside of this country haven't heard of Bradford. They're like, 'Where?' I'm like, 'Oh, forget it.' I just say I'm from London now! They seem happier with that. 'Oh yeah London, I've heard of that', and they write that down. If any of my mates from Bradford ever see this, I'm sorry! It's just the usual questions really, but it is going so well. People at the record company have told me that what's happening abroad is incredible. There are countries where my records are number one in the airplay charts and I've never even been there.

So far we've concentrated on Europe. I've worked really hard there. What's happening out there is just amazing, I've had a number one in Holland for three weeks, I've been really high in the charts in Germany and Spain and I've sold loads of records in Scandinavia.

When I go to a different country I have to start from scratch. They haven't seen *Pop Idol*, they don't know who I am, but the records are still getting played on the radio, and I'm getting covered in magazines. In Southeast Asia 'Anyone Of Us' has been the real breakthrough track. I've never been to Hong Kong, Korea, Japan or China so it's amazing how it's all come off. It's weird, because when I go there it will be like going back in time, because 'Anyone Of Us' came out ages ago here. On one level it's frustrating, because I'm trying to move on with my music and everything, but on another level it's just incredible. I think it's important that in these places I go back to the beginning and do it all again. I have to earn whatever I get, wherever I go. I never want to get complacent and just expect success without having to work hard for it.

My record company BMG had an international showcase in Dublin earlier this year. All the heads of all the different regions were there: from Asia, from Europe, even America. Clive Davis was there: he's one of the most famous record company people in America; he's the guy who discovered Whitney Houston and loads of others. He's a legend. L.A. Reid was there too. He's worked with TLC and loads of really cool artists. He's the guy who signed Pink. You know in her song, 'Don't Let Me, Get Me', she sings that line, 'L.A. told me, you'll be a pop star ...'? Well, that's L.A. Reid.

It was an acoustic set which was brilliant for me because I was able to show a wide range of what I'm able to do. The first song was 'Sentimental', which is one of the tracks from the first album that I wrote myself – I did that with a guitarist. It just sounded amazing. Then I played another two numbers.

The reaction was unbelievable, I walked off the stage and everyone was blown away, the heads of the Asian region were saying, 'You have to come over to Asia, you will be huge.' L.A. Reid said I was cool – to have someone who's worked with great R'n'B stars say that was amazing. The best one was Clive Davis. He said he was 'excited' at the prospect of me breaking America. Him excited – not half as excited as I was when he said that! He said he's got a track for me that will help me break America and I was like, my goodness, it's unreal!

I won't be rushing to break America though. A lot of really talented people have tried to do it and failed, so everything's got to be just right. Maybe this time next year. I'll have had two albums over here and hopefully I'll have started working on the third one. I don't want to release the first album in America, it won't work there. Before I even think about America, I have to go to Asia and keep working Europe. The single most important place to me will always be this country because this is where my heart is and where my best fans are. I'll never ignore my UK fans, no matter how things go in other parts of the world.

'I never want to get complacent and just expect success without having to work for it'

Northwest London, 26 May 2003. It's Bank Holiday Monday, the hottest day of the year so far, and most of the UK seems to be strolling around without a care in the world, sucking on ice lollies and soaking up the sun. Gareth and I are squeezed into his press officer's sporty two-seater car, with the engine off, the roof shut and the windows all the way up. It's sweltering. Gareth is in the passenger seat. He's sweating. He's wearing a green camouflage style T-shirt, jeans, dark blue trainers and a black cap. On his lap is a load of recordable CDs with song titles scrawled on them in black ink. Some are songs that Gareth has written himself, some have been written for him. Gareth keeps turning the volume up 'just a bit louder' until the car is actually vibrating and passers-by are straining their necks to see what kind of weirdos shut themselves in a car when it's over eighty degrees.

Gareth is enjoying himself, singing along and pointing out piano breaks, guitar parts and drum patterns that he particularly likes. When he's not singing the lead, he's trying out harmonies, and more often than not, it works.

We listen to beautiful ballads (one is just Gareth and a piano, nothing else – it sounds incredible), cheeky R'n'B tracks, tracks with sexy guitar – and even though none of them are finished, they all sound amazing. Whether they make it on to the album or not is another matter, as Gareth explains when we finally get out of the hottest, loudest car in the world…

Making an album is a long process. You can work on songs for months before they're right. Some songs never get beyond the first version.

I've been doing a lot of writing myself. I write on my laptop computer, using a keyboard that plugs into it. It's brilliant because it means I can write at home, take the laptop into the studio and just plug it in. I've also got electronic drum pads, with a bass drum, cymbal and hi-hat and everything, so I don't actually need a recording studio or a record company!

I usually start with the drums, get the beat, then do the guitar parts, and start building up the layers. It's such an amazing feeling to go from nothing to a proper track. I'll be playing a lot of the instruments on the second album.

It's not the first time I've ever written songs: I had to do it for my GCSEs. It was always love songs about one girlfriend or another. I never wrote a song about sweets or wrestling or stuff like that! Maybe one day I'll release *Gareth – The Early Years*, the secret songs of Gareth Gates!

Gareth on…

STEVIE WONDER

I'm getting into people that other people have recommended I listen to. Stevie Wonder has been more of a recent discovery. He's a brilliant pianist, he's got the most beautiful voice and he's a genius songwriter.

MARK STEVENS

I've said before that there are some unbelievable musicians at my church. There's a guy there I've learned a lot from, an Australian guy called Mark Stevens. He's got one of the best voices that I've heard. He was an actor in *Neighbours* for years, he played someone called Nick Page. If you saw a picture of him, or on TV, you'd know him. He's incredible, he's been a real inspiration to me.

'It's important for me to be a bit more independent, write a lot more of my own stuff'

Gareth on...

ELVIS

Elvis is my ultimate, ultimate idol. He's the King – of everything! The music, the looks, he's just amazing. For me, he's the best looking man that ever lived, his eyes are just so striking. When I think of Elvis, I think of him dressed in a white suit from the Vegas years, like the one that I wore on tour, but with a younger face. Not with the big old sideburns. I'd love to look like him. When we were growing up, the only music that was played in my house more than Elvis was UB40. That's because my dad's from Birmingham and they're from Birmingham. Then it was Elvis, then Abba – I don't want to look like Abba!

This time round, when I'm writing, I'm imagining people dancing to my songs. The sort of songs that get me dancing are things like R'n'B and hip-hop, you know, like Nelly or Justin. That's the level that I'm pitching at. When I hear a song I like on the radio I take it to pieces in my head. Even the smallest sound like a rhythm, I think I could use that in some way. I don't sing along in a club out loud if a song I like comes on. I'm listening for sounds in the track, for the grooves, the drums, the bass. I go home and try and play what I've heard, imitate the grooves, then add my own style.

I've heard my music playing in shops and bars, but one of the things I want now is to hear my music played in clubs and see people dancing to it. I think if you played one of the singles from the first album in a club, the dance floor would just empty – whoosh! I'd be saying, 'Pleeeease come back and dance to "Anyone Of Us"!' Would I stay and dance? Would I, heck. I'd be embarrassed!

I'm really proud of the first album, but I want to move on now. All the things that I've done over the past year have been really important for me to get grounded in the business, but now it's important for me to be a bit more independent, write a lot more of my own stuff. I've grown up a lot in the last year. The people who liked the first album have grown up a bit too. Hopefully all the fans I have already will be happy with the new music and I'll get some new fans too.

I've mainly been recording in London, but I've also been working in Sweden and Norway. If I'm in a different country then in some ways it's easier to focus on recording because that's the sole reason I'm there. There's no pressure to finish something by a certain time just because there's something you want to see that night or someone's asked you to go out. I'm not easily distracted, because my work is the most important thing to me, but it's always in the back of my mind, 'If I work harder, or if I work quicker, or if I go without lunch, or if I finish early then I can see this person, or have a drink with my mates or whatever.'

I love recording; I'm a control freak in the studio. If something needs doing again and again and again, I'll do it. I work myself really hard. I can sing at any time, but I like to start in the morning so I've got the whole day to make sure it's perfect and not just OK.

Gareth on…

MICHAEL JACKSON

In the whole of my life I've only ever had two posters on my wall and one of them was Michael Jackson. It was a picture and it was a mirror as well. Classy, eh? It had a picture of him with a mask over his face. Hang on, was he wearing that? No, it was just his face. It had 'Michael Jackson' written on it as well. His videos are amazing as well. I love 'Bad', where they're all in the subway. Videos like that don't have loads of special effects, just brilliant performances. I'm not a fan of videos that look like they were made on a computer. I don't mind special effects like the ones in 'Thriller'. That's just make-up and great dancing. He's probably the only person I'd be nervous about meeting. I'd be completely star-struck because he's just awesome. Awesome. If I spent time with him, I'd just want to hang out, find out what he's really like. If he ever, ever wanted to be on a record with me, even if it was in ten years' time, I'd be like, yeah, without question. This is an open invitation! Michael, if you ever want to be on a record with me, ever, then that would be absolutely amazing.

Apart from Michael Jackson, I probably wouldn't want to work with a huge, huge star, because it might look like I was just using them to further my career. Having said that, I'd work with Britney. Who knows, it could happen! I'd be singing away, she'd be doing all her dancing. I'd really like to work with Christina Aguilera as well, she's such an amazing singer. I think our voices would really complement each other. Someone else I'd love to do a duet with is Pink. She's wicked.

Whatever the song is about, I've got to be feeling it. To make myself feel sad when I'm recording a sad song, I have an image in my head of what I think the song is about. I might think about a specific person, or about a specific experience. It's the same if I'm singing a sexy song, I have to get in the mood for that too. It's a lot easier to express yourself when you've written the song, because you know exactly what you're singing about. When you're writing it, the pictures in your mind are already there.

Now when I'm writing songs, I have a really clear idea in my mind of what I want the video to look like. I'm proud of the videos I've made so far and, if they come on the TV, I'm able to watch myself without getting embarrassed. Having said that, if I'm at home and I've got the remote, I'll probably switch over to the footie.

I want to get more involved in my videos. My favourite videos ever are probably Michael Jackson ones. In 'The Way You Make Me Feel', he's on the street with a girl and he's dancing away with his hands held out to her. That's the way that I want to be. If it means I have to dance more in my videos then, oh well, I'll have to try it! I'll probably just have the odd little move, rather than a full-on routine, because I'm crap at dancing really. I'm not an amazing mover to be honest, but I can learn. I've got a sense of rhythm at least! When you make a video, they can shoot a dance move ten times and use the best one. That's what I'm hoping for. If there are girls in my videos dancing with me, I want to be the one who picks them. I'd hold auditions where loads of fit girls would come in and dance in front of me. That would be a good day.

chips and kickboxing
– bits of chat with Gareth

'My ideal meal out would be a **romantic meal for two,** with **soft lighting and candles**'

I need to put weight on; to be honest I'm looking a bit weedy. I was doing a wicked kickboxing programme for about a month, but I was really busy round Europe so I had to stop. It's a shame because I was looking a lot better, my chest and arms were better, but now …

It's lunchtime and Gareth's eating 'big chips' in a posh restaurant near his management offices. It's the second 'healthy' meal he's had today. His mum is staying with him and made him a sausage sandwich before he left.

It's a glorious day, and we're sitting outside. Gareth has his 'stealth' outfit on: cap, jeans, nondescript T-shirt, but the thing that gives him away is his voice. Not the stammering but the volume. His broad Bradford accent booms out in between mouthfuls of chip (dipped in 'healthy' mayonnaise) – 'I do like my food.'

Since I've been living in London, I've been eating out quite a lot. I'm the kind of person who has the same things when I go to the same restaurants. I've got my favourite dishes and I stick to them. There are a handful of restaurants that I go to quite a lot. My ideal meal out would be a romantic meal for two, with soft lighting and candles. I don't like being spotted, so I might keep my hat on. It's not a crime to wear a cool hat indoors, is it? The one I had on in that paparazzi picture of me next to that lamppost is wicked in real life – honest.

For starters I'd have paté de foie gras (made from goose liver, yuk), with a bit of bread or that thin toast they do in posh restaurants. For main course I'd have steak with chips and salad. I always like it cooked medium. The type of steak I actually like best is Chateaubriand. Foie gras, Chateaubriand! I'm living the high life! With my speech, though, I'm a bit of a pointer at menus. If I was asking for Chateaubriand I'd be like, 'Shh, shh, shh, oh I'll have one of them!' and just point at it.

Usually I don't have much room for a big dessert so I'll just have a selection of sorbets. Coconut, banana, whatever – but always with vanilla ice cream. Always. That's a pretty good meal, isn't it? I'm hungry now just talking about it! I always drink champagne when I'm eating out. Always. I have changed, haven't I? I don't get the most expensive champagne in the restaurant. I like Laurent Perrier champagne, always with cassis, which turns the champagne a pinky red colour. It's called a Kir Royale. Sometimes when I'm sitting in a nice restaurant with all the fancy food around me I do think, 'Look at me!'

I wasn't always into fancy food. My favourite food growing up was burger and chips. I've always loved steak though. You know what gets me, though? You know scampi? The scampi at home in Bradford is a round shape, like a 10p, with batter on it – it's absolutely gorgeous, don't get me wrong, but the scampi down here in London looks more like a little banana – it's even got a tail and an eye! It's like a different thing entirely! That's funny!

I'm a really, really bad cook. I don't cook at all. I'm lucky because I have friends who are really good cooks, so I invite them round to dinner all the time. They know if they want to eat that they'll be doing the cooking! If I'm left to myself, it'd have to be Pot Noodle. I can cook a Pot Noodle.

CLOTHES

I do like buying clothes, even though I've got a stylist. I've always been a little bit of a poseur. I think it's because when me and my sister were really young we got dressed up to look exactly the same, the photos are outrageous. I started buying my own clothes as soon as I could, I think it was when I went to senior school, I would have been about twelve. I don't dress up special every day; most days I just dress to be comfortable – I throw a hat or a cap on, leave my hair all over the place. That's me. For everyday situations it takes five minutes to get ready, and that includes the shower! You know, put it on, get out. If I'm working on a TV show, or I'm having photos done, then my image has to be perfect for that. For a TV show, having to have make-up and hair done, deciding what I'm going to wear, takes about an hour. One good thing about being a solo artist is that I don't have to wait for other people to get ready all the time.

When I was younger, the labels I was into were Adidas, Reebok, Nike, but it's all changed now. I suppose the flashiest item of clothing I've got is my Gucci watch. I bought it myself. I wear it all the time. I'm not the kind of person who buys something just to keep it in a drawer or in the wardrobe. You have to wear these things!

'The *flashest item of clothing I've got is* **my Gucci watch**'

THE STUFF I BUY

The last thing I bought was the most recent series of *Friends* on DVD. I've got all the series apart from the first three or four. I don't think I'll get them because I didn't think it was all that funny at first. Out of all the *Friends* characters I'm definitely Joey: 'How you doin'?' He's brilliant. I fancy Rachel, obviously, but the best one to watch is Phoebe, she is just so funny. I love when she sings, 'Smelly cat, smelly cat, what are they feeding you?' She's a songwriting inspiration!

I've got tons of DVDs. Tons. The last film I got was *Minority Report* with Tom Cruise. It's absolutely amazing. The bits where he makes those screens come to life just by moving his hands round are brilliant. I've got a whole wall of DVDs, I just haven't got time to watch most of them.

The last CD I bought was probably Missy Elliott's *Under Construction*. It's wicked. I get given loads of CDs for nothing. I need to listen to what's going on, especially when I'm writing. I got given a huge bag of CDs, R'n'B, soul, everything. I haven't got time to listen to them all, but I do put a lot of stuff on my iPod.

Apart from CDs and DVDs, I don't really collect anything. When I was younger I used to collect WWF wrestling figures! How embarrassing! Me and my mates had loads of them. We used to build these little wrestling rings for them to fight in. The Ultimate Warrior was my favourite. He had this mask, and these tassels. We used to dress up like them and everything! It was wicked. I was mad into the Teenage Mutant Ninja Turtles too! I had loads of Turtles stuff. Do you remember their bandana mask things? Heroes in a half-shell they were … I had a real thing with anything to do with wrestling or fighting. I'm not bothered about it at all any more.

One show I did used to love was *Gladiators*. Apart from the Michael Jackson picture mirror thing, the only other picture I had on my wall when I was growing up was a framed picture of Jet from the Gladiators! Do you remember her? I used to proper fancy her. I think she was going out with one of the other Gladiators … In the picture she was wearing her pink lycra Gladiator outfit, she was so fit. It was quality. She'd probably beat me up if I ever went out with her – she'd have me for breakfast! My press officer told me she used to work with her. Apparently she's lovely. She's called Diane in real life.

I've kind of got used to the fact that I can buy load of things, but I never take it for granted.

Afterword
the future

On a personal level, I do want to get married and have kids one day. Maybe three kids? I grew up with loads of other kids around me, and I want my children to have that too. I haven't got any names yet, but I don't want any fancy names. I want normal names like John. 'Come here, John!' 'Put that down, John!' Not for a girl, though! I've got my dad's name as my middle name (Paul), so if I have a boy he might have Gareth as a middle name.

Everyone knows that before *Pop Idol* happened I was going to go to the Northern College of Music in Manchester to study to be an opera singer. It's something I really want to get back to when I'm older, in my late thirties maybe, something like that. I'd still be a tenor. I've always wanted to be in some huge opera show. I can picture myself doing that when I'm older. I'd need to work really hard to get my voice to that level. It would probably take me about six months of really hard work and practice to get back up to that level.

I've wanted to be a singer all my life and I'm still really, really ambitious. I want to be successful all over the world. I don't want to ignore the UK, but I do want to do as well as I can everywhere. Things have started off brilliantly, but it's a big world and there is still so much for me to achieve. I hope that this is only the beginning.